GUT BUSTERS

OVER
600 JOKES
THAT PACK
A PUNCH...LINE!

FROM THE LAUGH FACTORY

APPLESAUCE PRESS

This book may be ordered by mail from the publisher. Please include $2.95 for postage and handling. Please support your local bookseller first!

Books published by Cider Mill Press Book Publishers are available at special discounts for bulk purchases in the United States by corporations, institutions, and other organizations. For more information, please contact the publisher.

Applesauce Press is an imprint of
Cider Mill Press Book Publishers
"Where good books are ready for press"
12 Port Farm Road
Kennebunkport, Maine 04046

Visit us on the Web!
www.cidermillpress.com

Design by Tilly Grassa - TGCreative Services
All illustrations courtesy of Anthony Owsley

1 2 3 4 5 6 7 8 9 0
First Edition

CONTENTS

CHAPTER
1
Elephunnies

What did Tarzan say when he saw three elephants wearing sunglasses? Nothing. He didn't recognize them.

* *

How did an elephant get stuck in a tree?
His parachute got caught.

How do you know when an invisible elephant is behind you?
You'll smell the peanuts on his breath.

WHAT MAKES AN ELEPHANT FEEL SICK?
A PACHYGERM.

What's gray, carries flowers, and visits sick people?
A get wellephant.

What did the label on the back of the elephant's designer jeans read?
Wide load.

WHAT HAS A TRUNK, WEIGHS TWO TONS, AND IS RED ALL OVER?
AN ELEPHANT WITH A BAD SUNBURN.

What climbs trees, buries nuts, and weighs two tons?
An elephant who thinks he's a squirrel.

What did the polite elephant on the subway do?
He stood up and let five ladies take his seat.

What do you get if you cross a prehistoric elephant and a flock of sheep?
A very woolly mammoth.

How do you know there's an elephant in the refrigerator?
Footprints in the butter.

How do you get an elephant in the refrigerator?
Open the door, put in the elephant, and then close the door.

HOW DO YOU KNOW THERE ARE TWO ELEPHANTS IN THE REFRIGERATOR?
YOU HEAR GIGGLING WHEN YOU CLOSE THE DOOR.

How can you tell when an elephant is hiding in your closet?
You won't be able to get the door shut.

• •

What's gray and bounces?
An elephant on a trampoline.

WHAT'S GRAY, WEIGHS 2,000 POUNDS, AND FLOATS?
AN ELEPHANT WEARING A LIFE JACKET.

• •

What has two wheels, giant ears, and wobbles?
An elephant learning to ride a bike.

• •

Can elephants fly?
Yes. But only if they have a pilot's license.

HOW DO YOU MAKE AN ELEPHANT FLOAT?
POUR SODA INTO A GLASS, ADD A SCOOP
OF ICE CREAM, AND DUMP IN AN ELEPHANT.

● ● ● ● ● ● ● ● ● ● ● ● ● ● ● ● ● ●

What's gray, has big ears, and weighs 500 pounds? A very obese mouse.

● ● ● ● ● ● ● ● ● ● ●

Where's the best place to watch an elephant pole vault?
As far away from the landing pit as possible.

HOW DID THE ELEPHANT GET HIS TRUNK
STUCK IN THE DRAINPIPE?
HE PUT HIS NOSE WHERE IT DIDN'T
BELONG.

What did the peanut vendor say to the elephant?
Keep your nose out of my business.

What do elephants wear on the beach?
Bathing trunks.

* *

Why did the elephant wear blue tennis shoes?
Because his white ones always get dirty.

* * * * * * * *

Why do cowboys ride horses instead of elephants?
Elephants take too long to saddle.

Why don't Eskimos keep elephants as pets?
Elephants can't squeeze into igloos.

▲▲▲▲▲▲▲▲▲▲▲▲▲▲▲▲▲▲▲▲▲▲▲▲▲▲▲▲▲▲

WHAT DO ELEPHANTS BRING TO A SAUNA BATH?
SWIMMING TRUNKS.

▼▼▼▼▼▼▼▼▼▼▼▼▼▼▼▼▼▼▼▼▼▼▼▼▼▼▼▼▼▼

Why didn't Mr. Elephant get rich?
He always agreed to work for peanuts.

What has red lips, five tongues, and a trunk?
A girl elephant wearing lipstick and sneakers.

WHAT'S BLUE, HAS BIG EARS, AND WEIGHS TWO TONS.
A SPOILED ELEPHANT HOLDING ITS BREATH.

▲▲▲▲▲▲▲▲▲▲▲▲▲▲▲▲▲▲▲▲▲▲▲▲▲▲▲▲▲▲

Why do elephants have white tusks?
They brush after every meal.

How do you make a gray elephant blue? Tell him a sad story.

How do you can an elephant? Just say, "You're fired!"

What do you get if you cross pachyderms with tiny insects? Eleph-ants.

Man: I used to have a pet elephant, but I had to get rid of him.
Guy: Why?
Man: I was spending too much time cleaning out the litter box.

What do you get if you cross an elephant and a turtle?
I don't know; but you should see the size of its shell.

• • • • • • • • • • • • • • • • • •

WHAT DO YOU GET WHEN AN ELEPHANT STEPS ON A CAN OF CORN?
CREAMED CORN.

• • • • • • • • • •

What weighs two tons and has a million red dots on it?
An elephant with the measles.

• • • • • • • • • • •

What's as big as an elephant, looks like an elephant, but doesn't weigh an ounce?
An elephant's shadow.

WHAT DO YOU GET IF YOU CROSS A
CENTIPEDE AND AN ELEPHANT?
YOU GET OUT OF THE WAY!

* * * * * * * * * * * * * * * * *

Why do elephants have trunks?
Because they'd look ridiculous with
suitcases on their faces.

A man took his trained elephant to the circus.
"Dance," he said as the band began to play.
Instantly, the elephant began to dance around as
the owner of the circus watched closely. When
the number ended, the trained turned to the
circus owner. "Well," he said, "are we hired?"
"No," replied the circus owner. The trainer was
stunned. "Why not?" he asked. "Because," the
circus owner snapped, "the band played a waltz
and your elephant did a mamba."

* *

What do you get if you cross an
elephant with a mouse?
I don't know, but it makes big
holes in the wall.

Barry: Why do elephants paint themselves purple?
Larry: I don't know.
Barry: So they can hide on grapevines.
Larry: I've never seen an elephant on a grapevine.
Barry: That's because they do such a good job.

* * * * * * * * * * * * * * * * * *

WHAT'S GRAY, HAS
BIG EARS, AND IS
TEN FEET TALL?
A MOUSE ON STILTS.

* * * * * * * * * *

Ike: I went on safari in Africa and late one night I shot an elephant in my pajamas.
Spike: Don't be ridiculous! How could an elephant fit in your pajamas?

* *

Why do elephants make fantastic reporters?
They have a great nose for news.

* *

HOW CAN YOU TELL IF AN ELEPHANT IS SNOBBY?
A SNOBBY ELEPHANT WALKS AROUND WITH ITS NOSE STUCK UP IN THE AIR.

Boy: Are peanuts fattening?
Girl: Have you ever seen a skinny elephant?

* *

CHAPTER
2
Lunchtime Laughs

WHY WASN'T THE ASTRONAUT'S
SON IN THE CAFETERIA?
HE WENT HOME FOR LAUNCH.

• •

Where does
Jack Frost
sit in the
cafeteria?
With the
cool kids.

• •

Teacher #1: I usually skip lunch and jog instead.
Teacher #2: I jog at lunchtime, too, but I eat
on the run.

• •

**NOTICE: The food at the medical
school cafeteria is so bad that
with every meal you get a free
prescription!**

What do you get if a ghost flies into the school cafeteria?
A food fright.

Where do math teachers go for their noonday meal?

To a lunch counter.

Teacher: If you had six potatoes to divide between twelve people. What would you do?
Student: Mash the potatoes.

Principal: Why are you late for school?
Student: I'm not late for school, I'm early for lunch.

WHAT DO MEMBERS OF THE SCHOOL BASEBALL TEAM EAT THEIR LUNCHES ON?
HOME PLATES.

WHEN DOES A SANDWICH ASK A LOT OF QUESTIONS? WHEN IT'S MADE WITH WHY BREAD.

Why?

What does a horn player use to brush his teeth?
A tuba toothpaste.

SIGN IN A SCHOOL LUNCHROOM:
Ask for our senior discount.

Student #1: What's the best thing to have in our school cafeteria?
Student #2: A brown-bag lunch.

HOW DID THE PLATE GET A CRACK IN IT?

IT HAD A LUNCH BREAK.

The food in our school cafeteria is so bad the mice order takeout lunches.

What do dance school students drink with their lunches?
Tap water.

What did the clumsy student say after he spilled his soup?

Don't worry everyone, lunch is on me.

KNOCK! KNOCK!
WHO'S THERE?
MISTER E.
MISTER E. WHO?
MISTER E. MEAT IS WHAT THEY'RE SERVING FOR LUNCH TODAY.

What do you call a young Scot who works in a school cafeteria?
The lunch laddie.

▲▲▲▲▲▲▲▲▲▲

Teacher: I'd like to know what's in the stew you're serving for lunch today.
Cook: Oh, no you wouldn't.

▼▼▼▼▼▼▼▼▼▼

What did the Abominable Snowman Lunch Lady serve to her students?
Cold cuts.

WHICH IS THE BEST DAY OF THE WEEK TO SERVE HAMBURGERS FOR LUNCH?
FRY DAY.

What did the school bowling team order for lunch?

Spare ribs.

▲▲▲▲▲▲▲▲▲▲▲▲▲▲▲▲▲▲▲▲▲▲▲▲▲▲▲▲▲▲

What's a grumpy salad made with?

Lettuce alone.

▼▼▼▼▼▼▼▼▼▼▼▼▼▼▼▼▼▼▼▼▼▼▼▼▼▼▼▼▼▼

What kind of cheese did the lunch lady serve to the school basketball team?

Swish cheese.

▼▼▼▼▼▼▼▼▼▼▼▼▼▼▼▼▼▼▼▼▼▼▼▼▼▼▼▼▼▼

What kind of cake should you never eat for dessert?

A cake of soap.

▲▲▲▲▲▲▲▲▲▲▲▲▲▲▲▲▲▲▲▲▲▲▲▲▲▲▲▲▲▲

What is a down-to-earth sandwich made of?

Ground beef.

What did the geometry teacher have for lunch?
A square meal.

What did the slice of bread say to the sweet roll?
Will you be my honeybun?

WHAT IS AN AUTHOR'S SANDWICH MADE OF?
LOTS OF BALONEY ON WRITE BREAD.

Where's the worst place to sit in the school cafeteria?
At the cruel kids' table.

What did the tennis player say to the lunch lady?
What are you serving today?

Why did the school principal hire a tightrope walker to prepare lunch? He wanted her students to have balanced meals.

New Teacher: Do they have good food in the school cafeteria?
Old Teacher: Yes. Until somebody cooks it.

COOK: I'M TIRED OF EVERYONE KIDDING ME ABOUT THE MEALS I SERVE.
PRINCIPAL: DON'T TAKE OFFENSE. THEY'RE JUST TASTELESS JOKES.

How did the butter knife get into trouble in the cafeteria?
It kept cutting up at the lunch table.

**Why did the student eat
a five-dollar bill?**
**His mother told him it was
his lunch money.**

WHAT DO YOU GET IF YOU EAT YOUR
LUNCH TOO FAST?

A MEAL TICKET.

What did the leopard say to the lion
when the lunch bell rang?
Save me a spot at our table.

**Why did the student
throw his lunch
in the garbage?**
**It was nothing but
junk food.**

Knock! Knock!
Who's there?
Sieve.
Sieve who?
Sieve me a seat in
the lunchroom.

What did the Drivers' Ed teacher have for lunch?
Park chops.

What did the math teachers do in the cafeteria?
They divided their lunches among them.

LUNCH LADY: WHY DO YOU HAVE A PICKLE BEHIND YOUR EAR?
DORK STUDENT: OH NO! I MUST HAVE EATEN MY PENCIL!

Student: For crying out loud! Are we having alphabet soup for lunch again?
Lunch Lady: Yes. Read it and weep.

Why did the dog go to school at noon?
He was part of the flea lunch program.

* * * * * * * * * * * * * * * *

WHY WAS THE MATH TEACHER OVERWEIGHT?
EVERY DAY AT LUNCH HE ADDED A FEW POUNDS.

* * * * * * * * * * * * * * *

Why did the student bring scissors into the cafeteria?
He wanted to cut the lunch line.

* * * * * * * * * * * * * * * * * * *

Boy: Does this cafeteria food taste as bad as it looks?
Girl: No. It tastes worse.

Knock! Knock!
Who's there?
Hiatus.
Hiatus who?
Hiatus lunch and now the school bully is after me.

CHAPTER **3**

Zombies, Werewolves & Vampires

Why did Mrs. Zombie join a monster health club?
She was starting to lose her ghoulish figure.

BORIS: DOES MRS. ZOMBIE'S WEDDING RING HAVE A DIAMOND IN IT?
IGOR: NO. IT HAS A TOMBSTONE.

What did the boy zombie say to the pretty girl zombie?
I've been dying to go out with you.

What game do zombie kids like to play?
Corpse and robbers.

What's one thing a zombie can never be at a social gathering?
The life of the party.

BOY ZOMBIE: IF YOU DON'T GO OUT WITH ME, I'LL JUST DIE.

GIRL ZOMBIE: IT'S A LITTLE LATE FOR THAT.

- -

NOTICE:
Zombie appliances don't come with a lifetime guarantee.

- - - - - - - - - - - -

What happens when a zombie graduates from college?
Everyone mourns his passing.

- -

When did the fisherman become a zombie?

When he reached the end of the line.

- -

Knock! Knock!
Who's there?
Zombies.
Zombies who?
Zombies gather honey while others guard the hive.

Where do zombies reside?
On dead end streets.

● ● ● ● ● ● ● ● ● ● ● ● ●

WHEN DID THE
HAIRDRESSER BECOME
A ZOMBIE?
AFTER SHE DYED.

● ● ● ● ● ● ● ● ● ● ● ●

When did the
football player
become a zombie?
After he kicked off.

● ● ● ● ● ● ● ● ● ● ● ● ● ● ● ● ●

When did the frogman become a zombie?
After he croaked.

● ● ● ● ● ● ● ● ● ● ● ● ● ● ● ● ● ● ●

WHEN DID THE DOOR MAKER
BECOME A ZOMBIE?
AFTER HE GOT KNOCKED OFF.

What happened when a vampire bumped
into the Abominable Snowman?
Frost bite.

When did the quarterback
become a zombie?
After he passed.

When did the cowboy
become a zombie?
After the
last roundup.

When did the
jogger become a
zombie?
After his final
race was run.

When did the desk clerk become a zombie?
After he checked out for the last time.

WHAT DID THE SURFER SAY AS HE
WATCHED THE WEREWOLF RUN AWAY?
HAIRY BACK, DUDE!

When does a werewolf feel depressed?
Once in a blue moon.

* * * * * * * * *

How did the
Wolfman get
to be a CEO?
He clawed
his way to
the top.

WOOF

* * * * * * * * * *

**How many parents does
the Wolfman have?**
One maw and four paws.

Knock! Knock!
Who's there?
Wendy.
Wendy who?
Wendy full moon rises, werewolves
start to prowl around.

SIGN ON A CLOSED WEREWOLF STORE:
Dog gone for the day.

* * * * * * * * * * * * * *

What should you use when you change a baby werewolf's diaper?
Flea powder.

* *

Where do you store wolfmen?
In a werehouse.

* *

What do you get if you cross King Kong with a werewolf?
A giant, very hairy beast that goes ape when the full moon rises.

* *

WANTED: HORROR WRITER NEEDED TO PEN HAIR-RAISING TALES FOR BALD WEREWOLF.

What do you call a
metric werewolf?
The liter of the pack.

Dracula: **Tonight there's a full
moon. Tomorrow there isn't.**
Wolfman: **Oh well. Hair today.
Gone tomorrow.**

SHOW ME A WOLFMAN ABOUT TO BE
MARRIED...AND I'LL SHOW YOU A
DOG GROOMER.

Which werewolf
works for the
post office?
The Alpha
mail carrier.

What happened to
the vampire grape
who got caught out
in the sun?
He turned into a raisin.

When does Dracula visit with his children's teachers?
On bat-to-school night.

● ● ● ● ● ● ● ● ● ● ● ● ● ● ● ● ● ● ●

Vampire: How much did you pay for the lining in the bottom of your coffin?
Dracula: I got it dirt cheap.

● ● ● ● ● ● ● ● ● ● ● ● ● ● ● ● ● ● ●

What do you call a two-headed vampire? A twilight double header.

WHEN DO VAMPIRES ATTACK GEEKS AND DWEEBS?
ON DORK NIGHTS.

Villager 1: Do you think we can burn down Dracula's castle and get away with it?
Villager 2: Yes. But it'll be a torch and go situation.

Show me a vampire who loves to play golf ... and I'll show you a monster who enjoys night clubbing.

• • • • • • • • • • • • • • • • • • • •

WHICH VAMPIRE WHINES TOO MUCH?

POUT DRACULA.

• • • • • • • • • • • • • • • • •

Why did the girl go to the doctor after her date with Dracula? He gave her a sore throat.

• • • • • • • • • • • •

Boris: Why is that baby vampire chewing on your neck?
Bride of Dracula: He's teething.

• • • • • • • • • • • • • • • • • • • •

What makes an African vampire bat very happy?
Flying into a herd of giraffes.

• • • • • • • • • • • • • • • • • • •

Igor: Why are you doing somersaults?
Vampire: I'm training to be an acro-bat.

WHAT DO YOU GET IF YOU CROSS A
VAMPIRE BAT WITH A PIG?
A HAMPIRE.

Why did the vampire take
an art class?
He wanted to learn how to
draw blood.

What is Santa Vampire's favorite
kind of blood?
Type O-O-O.

Why did the
vampire bat fly
into a cave?
She wanted to
hang out with
her friends.

CHAPTER
4
Jokey Jobs

What do you call a mean guy who chops down trees?
A lumberjerk.

▲▲▲▲▲▲▲▲▲▲▲▲

What's very quiet and cleans streets?
A mime sweeper.

▼▼▼▼▼▼▼▼▼▼▼▼

WHY DID THE FARMER PLAY HIS GUITAR IN THE CORNFIELD.
IT WAS MUSIC TO HIS EARS.

▼▼▼▼▼▼▼▼▼▼▼▼▼▼▼▼▼▼▼▼▼▼▼▼▼▼

What do disc jockey surfers ride?
Radio waves.

What do you get if you cross an athlete with a road construction worker?
A jock hammer.

DAFFY DEFINITIONS:
YACHT OWNERS - SUCCESSFUL SAILSMEN.
FISHING GEAR VENDORS - REEL ESTATE AGENTS.

▲▲▲▲▲▲▲▲▲▲▲▲▲▲▲▲▲▲▲▲▲▲▲▲▲▲▲▲

Do parsons and ministers get prayed vacations?

▼▼▼▼▼▼▼▼▼▼▼▼▼▼▼▼▼▼▼▼▼▼▼▼▼▼▼▼▼▼

When do lumberjacks kick back and relax?
On tree-day weekends.

▼▼▼▼▼▼▼▼▼▼▼▼▼▼▼▼▼▼▼▼▼▼▼▼▼▼▼▼▼▼

What do you get if you cross a rock and an employee? A hard worker.

▲▲▲▲▲▲▲▲▲▲▲▲▲▲▲▲▲▲▲▲▲▲▲▲▲▲▲▲

NOTICE: Sir Lancelot works the knight shift.

MIME -
A PERSON WHO IS
LOST FOR WORDS.

▼▼▼▼▼▼▼▼▼▼▼

Rick: I produce
calendars for
a living.
Nick: Oh! So you're a day worker.

▲▲▲▲▲▲▲▲▲▲▲▲▲▲▲▲▲▲▲▲▲▲▲▲▲▲▲▲▲▲▲▲▲▲

KNOCK! KNOCK!
WHO'S THERE?
COMMA.
COMMA WHO?
COMMA IN FOR A JOB INTERVIEW.

▼▼▼▼▼▼▼▼▼▼▼▼▼▼▼▼▼▼▼▼▼▼▼▼▼▼▼▼▼▼▼

Boy: I work in costumes at
Disney World.
Girl: What do you do?
Boy: I have a Mickey Mouse job.

Why did the fisherman go to the Anglers' Conference?
To do some networking.

A young man was applying for a job as a magician with a circus. "What's your best trick?" asked the owner of the show. "It's sawing a woman in half," boasted the young performer. "Isn't that a difficult trick?" asked the owner. "Not really," answered the magician. "I first started performing it on my sisters." "Do you come from a large family," asked the circus owner. The magician smiled. "I have six half sisters."

LUGGAGE MAKER – A case worker.

• •

Why did the teller stand next to the bank vault?
She wanted to be on the safe side.

How does an acrobat read a magazine?
He flips through the pages.

What do you call a necktie salesman who earns a million dollars?
A tycoon.

WHAT DID THE CLOCK MAKER SAY
TO THE REVOLUTIONARY SOLDIER?
GIVE ME A MINUTE, MAN.

What's the best way to avoid taxes?
Take a quick right at New Mexico.

What is a truck driver's favorite paint?
Semi-gloss.

ZACK: WHAT DO YOU DO AT THE CLOCK FACTORY?

MACK: I MAKE FACES.

* * * * * * * *

Then there was the politician who fired his writers and ended up speechless.

* * * * * * * * * * * *

How's your job at the peanut plant? The work is driving me nuts.

How's your job at the fan factory? It's a breeze.

* * * * * * * * * * * * * * * * *

How's your job at the school textbook company? I'm getting promoted.

HOW'S YOUR JOB AT THE STEAK KNIFE PLANT?

THEY'RE CUTTING BACK MY HOURS.

What happens when a steamship gets angry? It blows its stack.

Pirate #1: How much did you pay for your earrings?

Pirate #2: A buccaneer.

Tino: I flip pizzas for a living and the pay is good.

Gino: But isn't that a kind of a pie-in-the sky job?

* * * * * * * * * * * * * * * * * * * *

WHEN DO POP SINGERS GO BANKRUPT?
WHEN THEY HIT ROCK BOTTOM.

What do you get if you cross combat soldiers with a church choir? Battle hymns.

Doctor: The check you gave me last week came back.
Patient: So did the pain in my back you treated me for.

A hypochondriac told his doctor he was certain he had a fatal disease. "Nonsense," scolded the doctor. "You wouldn't know if you had that. With that particular disease there's no discomfort of any kind." "Oh no!" gasped the patient. "Those are my symptoms exactly!"

Man: My psychologist is a real wise guy. He encourages me to speak freely and then he charges me for listening.

Millie: Do you like selling pillows for a living?
Tillie: Yes. It's a soft job.

DOPEY DOCTORS' NAMES
Dr. Euell B. Fine
Dr. Noah Payne
Dr. Hope N. Wide
Dr. Ivanna Secondopinion
Nurse Dee Patients
Nurse Anita Doctor

What did the tired auctioneer say?
I'm going back to bid.

CHAPTER **5**

Peculiar People

What does Pirate Santa yell when he wants to raise the anchor?
Heave Ho Ho Ho!

• • • • • • • • • • • • • • •

What famous English sea captain had feathers?
Sir Francis Drake.

• • • • • • • • •

HOW DOES TARZAN KNOW EXACTLY HOW LONG EACH VINE IS?
BECAUSE TARZAN IS THE RULER OF THE JUNGLE.

• • • • • • • • • • • • • • • • •

Does Tarzan like rock and roll?
No. He's crazy about old time swing music.

• • • • • • • • • • • • • • • • •

What did Tarzan give his son for his birthday?
A swing set.

Who is the best athlete in Mother Goose Land?
Jock be nimble. Jock be quick.

What did the bad golfer say when he went into the pizza place?
I'll have my usual slice.

What do you say when you meet an angel?
Halo.

* *

What is Mr. Jam's favorite song?
For He's a Jelly Good Fellow.

• •

Why did the old lady who lived in the shoe get evicted from Mother Goose Land?
She couldn't foot her bills.

Beautician: Would you like a truth hairstyle?
Girl: What's that?
Beautician: I'll let you have it straight.

• • • • • • • • • • • • • • • • • •

WHAT DO YOU
GET IF YOU
CROSS A
VIKING AND A
LUMBERJACK?
A PERSON
WHO USES A
BATTLEAXE.

Lady: Why did you contact our online dating service, sir?
Guy: I'd like some miss information.

FRAN: WHAT DO YOU CALL JUDGE COBRA?
DAN: HISS HONOR.

▲▲▲▲▲▲▲▲▲▲▲▲▲▲▲▲▲▲▲▲▲▲▲▲▲▲▲▲▲▲▲

Why did 007 dye his hair yellow?
He wanted to be James Blond.

▲▲▲▲▲▲▲▲▲▲▲

WHAT DID THE
TIN MAN SAY
WHEN HE WAS
CAUGHT IN A
CLOUDBURST?
THIS IS VERY
RUSTFUL.

▼▼▼▼▼▼▼▼▼▼▼

A rich father turned to his teenage
daughter and smiled. "Honey, which
would you rather have for your
sixteenth birthday, a diamond necklace
or a trip to Paris?" The daughter
smiled back at her dad. "Let's go
to Paris," said she. "I heard diamond
necklaces are cheaper there."

Wife: I'm sending you to a psychologist to an analyzed.
Husband: I won't take this lying down.

▲▲▲▲▲▲▲▲▲▲▲▲▲▲▲▲▲▲▲▲▲▲▲▲▲▲▲▲

What is the name of a famous pirate fairy tale?
Booty and the Beast.

▼▼▼▼▼▼▼▼▼▼▼▼▼▼▼▼▼▼▼▼▼▼▼▼▼▼▼▼▼

Where did Captain Hook get a tattoo?
On his pirate chest.

▲▲▲▲▲▲▲▲▲▲▲▲▲▲▲▲▲▲▲▲▲▲▲▲▲▲▲▲

Who takes care of sailors on payday?
The check mate.

▼▼▼▼▼▼▼▼▼▼▼▼▼▼▼▼▼▼▼▼▼▼▼▼▼▼▼▼▼

WHO TAKES THE SHIP'S CREW JOGGING?
THE RUNNING MATE.

What did Romeo Crow say to Juliet Crow?
I just cawed to say I love you.

* * * * * * * * * * * * * * *

How does Sir Lancelot put money in the bank?

He uses a knight deposit box.

WHY ISN'T CINDERELLA A GOOD SOFTBALL PLAYER? SHE ALWAYS RUNS AWAY FROM THE BALL.

WHAT'S IT LIKE TO BE A MOM?

... you spend a lot of time kidding around.

... the job isn't all child's play.

... you have to baby everyone but yourself.

... you work from son up to son down.

... you have to know more than a daughter who knows everything.

... you have to look young, act young and think young while doing the same old things day after day.

* *

What is Pinocchio's favorite game?
Stickball.

* * * * * * * * * * * * * * * * * *

WHAT DID GEPPETTO GET WHEN HE SHOOK HANDS WITH PINOCCHIO? SPLINTERS.

What does Pinocchio spread on his toast?
Log jam.

What do you call four singing Pinocchios?
A string quartet.

WHY DID CAPTAIN KIRK SIT ON THE TREE STUMP? IT WAS THE CAPTAIN'S LOG.

• • • • • • • • • •

Pirate: How much is your corn?
Farmer: A buck an ear.

• • • • • • • • •

Who's the smartest fairy in Neverland?
Thinkerbell.

• •

Man: You called for a substitute store Santa so I rushed right over here.
Owner: Phew! You arrived in the St. Nick of time.

• •

What tune does Pinocchio play on the piano?
Chopsticks.

What goes whoosh! Ho! Ho! Yeow!? Santa sliding down a chimney with a fire in it.

What nationality is Santa Claus?
North Polish.

WHAT DID SANTA SHOUT WHEN HE GOT INTO HIS SLEIGH AND FOUND ONE REINDEER WAS MISSING?
"NO COMET!"

Why did Superman run super fast from one place to another?
He was in a no fly zone.

What do you call a group of superheroes who are bodybuilders?
The Flex Men.

* *

WHAT HAPPENED WHEN BATMAN'S PARTNER TURNED TO A LIFE OF CRIME?

HE CHANGED HIS NAME TO ROBIN HOOD.

* * * * * * * * * * * *

Why did Scrooge wear a hat made of dollar bills? Because he liked to keep money on his mind.

* * * * * * * * * * * * * * *

Hero #1: I can soar like an eagle.
Hero #2: I have the eyes of a hawk.
Hero #3: Shut up, bird brains.

* *

Which sheep is a mutant superhero?
Woolverine.

Spidey: Dude, should I hit this golf shot with a driver?
Big Hulk: No. Use an iron, man.

* *

Who is the North Pole's most famous celebrity after Santa Claus? Frosty the Showman.

* *

HEROINE: STOP WHERE YOU ARE, CROOK. I'M THE INVISIBLE GIRL AND I'M ARRESTING YOU.
ROBBER: I DON'T SEE THAT HAPPENING.

Which hero fixes leaky pipes and broken windows? The Building Super.

Why is the superhero Flash never sick very long?
He always has a speedy recovery.

* * * * * * * * * * * * * * * *

KNOCK! KNOCK!
WHO'S THERE?
I'M MIGHTY THOR.
I'M MIGHTY THOR WHO?
I'M MIGHTY THOR AND I NEED A
GOOD CHIROPRACTOR.

* * * * * * * * * * * * * * * *

CHAPTER
6
Animal Crack-ups

What's gray, weighs 2,000 pounds and spins around like a top?
A hippo stuck in a revolving door.

ATTENTION: Moles sell houses hole sale.

● ●

What weighs two tons and is gray and lumpy?
A hippo with the mumps.

● ●

WHY DO CHAMELEONS MAKE GREAT PARTY GUESTS?

BECAUSE THEY ALWAYS BLEND IN.

What do you get if you cross an antelope with a journalist?
A gnus reporter.

What's black and white and slowly turning blue?
A very cold penguin.

Why do leopards wear spotted coats?
The tigers bought all the striped ones.

• • • • • • • • • • •

WHY WAS THE LION
DRIPPING WET?
HE HAD A WATER
MANE BREAK.

• •

ATTENTION:
Wild hogs tell boaring
stories.

• •

What does a polar bear wear when his
head is cold?
An ice cap.

What do you get if you cross frogs
with chameleons?
Leapin' lizards.

What do you get if you cross a hippo with a hog?
The world's biggest pork chops.

WHAT DO YOU GET IF YOU CROSS A SHEEP AND A LARGE PRIMATE?
A BAH-BOON.

What do you call a dapper king of the jungle?
A dandy lion.

What do you get if you cross a coyote and a chimp?
A howler monkey.

WHAT DO YOU GET IF YOU SPILL BOILING WATER DOWN A RABBIT HOLE?
HOT CROSS BUNNIES.

What kind of exercises do bunnies do?
Hareobics.

▲▲▲▲▲▲▲▲▲▲▲▲

What theory did the famous skunk philosopher propose?
I stink, therefore I am.

▼▼▼▼▼▼▼▼▼▼▼▼▼▼▼▼▼▼▼▼▼▼▼▼▼▼

Where did the actor skunk deliver his monologue?
Scenter stage.

▼▼▼▼▼▼▼▼▼▼▼▼▼▼▼▼▼▼▼▼▼▼▼▼▼▼

ATTENTION: Rabbits like to rent garden apartments.

What do space squirrels like to eat?
Astronuts.

WHAT DO YOU GET IF YOU CROSS MINKS AND PINES?

VERY EXPENSIVE FUR TREES.

What do you get when a bunny marries Bambi?

Hare deer everywhere.

Show me two skunks who enlist in the Marine Corps, and I'll show you a phew good men.

WHAT DO YOU CALL A GRIZZLY THAT SHEDS?

BEAR NAKED.

What lives in an oak tree and cooks greasy meals?

A frying squirrel.

What's soggy and has large antlers?
A rain deer.

How do rabbits fly to Europe?
They take a hare plane.

• • • • • • • • • • • • • • • • • • • •

How much money do a dozen skunks have?
They have twelve scents.

How can you tell if a tree is a dogwood?
Check out its bark.

• • • • • • • • • • • • • • • • • • • •

WHAT'S BLACK AND WHITE AND GREEN ALL OVER?

A SLOPPY SKUNK EATING PEA SOUP.

• • • • • • • • • • • • • • • • • • • •

Why couldn't the herd of deer buy dinner?
Because they only had one buck.

What did the judge say when lawyer skunk appeared before him?
Odor in the court.

● ● ● ● ● ● ● ● ● ● ● ● ● ● ● ● ● ● ● ●

HOW DO YOU GET RID OF
UNWANTED RABBITS?
USE HARE REMOVER.

● ● ● ● ● ● ● ● ● ● ● ● ● ● ● ● ● ● ●

What did Mr. Beaver say to the oak tree?
It's been nice gnawing you.

● ● ● ● ● ● ● ● ● ● ● ● ● ● ● ● ● ● ● ●

ATTENTION:
Skunks use smell phones.
Snake phones have crawler I.D.
Roadrunner phones have speed dial.

What's the slowest way to send a letter?
Snail mail.

Then there was the gopher publisher who printed an underground newspaper.

What did Ms. Frog wear on her feet?
Open toad shoes.

HOW DID MR. TURTLE PAY HIS BILLS?
HE SHELLED OUT CASH.

Which animal lives in the White House and eats fish?
The presidential seal.

What's the best way to save a frog's life?
Clamp his mouth shut so he can't croak.

WHAT DID JUDGE MOLE SAY TO THE GOPHER WITNESS?

REMEMBER TO TELL THE HOLE TRUTH.

* * * * * * * * * * * * * * * * * * * *

What's worse than buying mittens for an octopus?

Buying sneakers for a centipede.

* *

Why did the boy porcupine follow the girl porcupine everywhere she went?
He was stuck on her.

What does Bullwinkle Moose drink when he has an upset stomach?
Elk-o-seltzer.

Why was the little bunny in the timeout chair?
He was having a bad hare day.

* *

What do little frogs use to catch fish?
Tadpoles.

* * * * * *

What did one porcupine say to the other?
Quit needling me.

Quit needling me!

* * * * * * * * * * * * * * * *

MOTHER: WHY DID YOU TAKE YOUR GOLDFISH OUT OF THE BOWL?

BOY: HE NEEDS A BATH.

What happened to the frog that parked near a fire hydrant?
He got toad away.

Why did Mr. Mole risk all of
his poker chips on one hand?
Because he wanted to gopher broke.

* * * * * * * * * * * * * *

HOW DOES A SKUNK GET RID OF ODORS?
HE USES AN EX-STINK-GUISHER.

* * * * * * * * * * * * * *

What did the waiter say to the skunk?
May I please take your odor, sir?

* * * * * *

Why was the
lion king sad
and lonely?
He had no pride.

* * * * * *

NOTICE: Sane squirrels live in nut
houses.

What do you get if you cross a skunk with a hand grenade? A stink bomb.

* * * * * * * * * * * * * *

What kind of stories did Mrs. Rabbit tell her children at bedtime? Cotton tales.

* * * * * * * * * * * * * * *

ATTENTION: Mr. Frog has a bachelor pad at his pond.

* * * * * * * *

Which skunk girl went to a fancy ball? Scenterella.

* * * * * * * *

WHAT DO YOU CALL A SKUNK THAT CARVES FIGURES OUT OF WOOD? A WHITTLE STINKER.

WHAT DO YOU GET IF YOU CROSS A
HOT-AIR BALLOON WITH A SKUNK?
SMETHING THAT RAISES A STINK.

What has three ears and a
cotton tail?
A rabbit eating corn on the cob.

Why did Bambi fail his test?
His teacher didn't want to pass the buck.

**Do rabbits
use combs?**
No. They use
hare brushes.

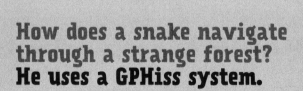

How does a snake navigate
through a strange forest?
He uses a GPHiss system.

ATTENTION: TURTLES ARE SHELLFISH REPTILES.

What did the little turtles say to their father?
You tortoise everything we know.

You tortoise everything we know

In which direction did the turtle move when he saw us watching him?
Tortoise.

MISS TORTOISE: HUMPH! YOU'RE A REAL SQUARE.
MR. TURTLE: WHAT DO YOU EXPECT? I'M A BOX TURTLE.

What do you call ...

A rodent's mate? A mouse spouse.

A tadpole's diary of his travels? A frog log.

A big rodent's rug? A rat mat.

Smokey's recliner? A bear chair.

Marty: Have you ever seen a coyote jog?

Artie: No, but I've seen a fox trot.

What do you get if you cross a rattlesnake with a car tire?
A snake that rattles and rolls.

What is a skunk's favorite holiday?
Scent Valentine's Day.

Which monkey can fly?
The hot-air baboon.

WHAT TIME IS IT
WHEN YOU SEE
A HIPPO SITTING
ON YOUR
DOGHOUSE?
TIME TO GET A
NEW DOGHOUSE.

What's black and white and slightly green?
A seasick zebra.

What's hairy and hops up and down?
A gorilla on a pogo stick.

WHAT DO YOU CALL A LION THAT GOBBLES UP YOUR FATHER'S SISTER?

AN AUNT EATER.

Lion: Do you want to race me?
Leopard: That depends. You're not a cheetah, are you?

What did the
boa say to
the python?
I have a
crush on you.

What's multi-colored,
slithers, and has a forked tongue?
A rainboa.

What do you get if you cross solar flares
and a leopard?
Sun spots.

* *

Why is it difficult for a giraffe to
apologize?
Because it takes a long time for a
giraffe to swallow its pride.

* *

HOW DOES A RHINO NAVIGATE
SAFELY ON A MISTY MORNING?
HE USES HIS FOG HORN.

What did Mr. Squirrel send his girlfriend when he joined he Army?
Forget-me-nuts.

What do you get if you cross a bison and a duck?
A buffalo bill.

WHICH JUNGLE ANIMAL IS ALWAYS POUTING?
A WHINOCEROS.

Which mink was a barbarian warrior?
Chinchilla the Hun.

Hunter: I spotted a leopard.
Guide: Baloney! They're born that way.

What did one duck football player say to the other duck football players?
Let's puddle up.

What do you get if you cross an octopus with a piece of furniture?
An arm, arm, arm, arm, arm, arm, arm, armchair.

Why do fish like to eat worms?
Who knows! They're just hooked on them.

* * * * * * * * * * * * * * * * * *

What happened when the lioness invited the tiger to dinner?
The tiger ate the lion's share of the food.

* * * * * * * * * * * * * * * * * *

WHAT DO YOU CALL AN ASIAN OX THAT TALKS TOO MUCH?
A YAKETY-YAK.

* *

Cowboy: I just saw a baby snake.
Cowgirl: How do you know it was a baby?
Cowboy: It had a rattle.

ANIMAL TONGUE TWISTERS

Lazy Larry Llama loves lovely Lacy Lion.

Timmy Turtle texted Tillie Tortoise ten times.

Hairy Harry Hound hurries home.

Sheep shouldn't sleep in shaky shacks.

Pretty Pinky Porker pines for Porky Peter Pointer.

Ron Watts runs rat races.

What animal can jump higher than the Empire State Building?
Any animal. The Empire State Building can't jump.

* * * * * * * * * * * * * * *

What do you get if you cross a turtle and an ATM machine?
A creature that shells out cash.

* * * * * * * * * * * * * * * *

What do you get if you cross a frog and a calendar?
Leap year.

WHAT FINANCIAL ADVICE DID MR. MOLE
GIVE TO MR. GOPHER?

DON'T BURROW MONEY.

****

What do you call an Arctic bear
that competes in
the Olympics?
A polar vaulter.

****

Who has lots
of long arms
and is a
western outlaw?

Billy the Squid.

****

WHAT DID MRS. SKUNK SAY TO MR.
SKUNK AT DINNERTIME?

CAN WE ODOR OUT TONIGHT?

What happens when silk worms race?
They usually end up in a tie.

Which monkey can't keep a secret?
The blaboon.

* *

Why did the pig farmer call the vet?
He wanted her to cure his ham.

• •

What happens when two frogs try to catch the same bug at the same time?
They end up tongue-tied.

• •

What's tiny, gray, has big ears, and a large trunk?
A mouse on a sea cruise.

* *

ANIMAL TRAINER #1: HOW'S THE GIRAFFE
                                 BUSINESS?
ANIMAL TRAINER #2: THINGS ARE LOOKING UP.

CHAPTER
7
Ditzes & Dorks

How do you write a letter to a dork?
Use the geek alphabet.

● ●

Mork: Did the doctor measure
your brain waves?
Dork: He couldn't. The tide was
too low.

● ●

MORK: I WAS BORN IN A HOSPITAL.
DORK: WHY? WERE YOU A SICKLY BABY?

● ●

Why did the dork feed his
cows money?
He wanted them to give
rich milk.

● ●

Why did the dork name his son
Cannon?
He wanted him to grow up to be
a big shot.

● ●

BILL: MY NAME SHOULD BE "DOOR."
JILL: WHY?
BILL: YOU'RE ALWAYS KNOCKING ME.

Why did the dork pour chicken broth on his car?
He wanted to soup up the motor.

Then there was the sick dork that thought he was a jock just because the doctor told him he had athlete's foot.

Reporter: Do you think women should have children after forty?
Dork: Heck no. Forty children are enough.

Joe: I'm glad I wasn't born in Germany.
Moe: Why?
Joe: I don't speak a word of German.

Mork: Do you remember your college days?
Dork: Sure. All ten of them.

Why did the dork put his bed in the fireplace?
He wanted to sleep like a log.

Al: The judge sentenced me to 200 years in jail.
Sal: Whew! You're lucky he didn't give you a life sentence.

WHY DID THE DORK BUY A FARM THREE MILES LONG AND THREE INCHES WIDE?
HE PLANNED TO RAISE SPAGHETTI.

Girl: You're a vegetable dork.
Boy: What does that mean?
Girl: You have a bean brain.

What did the dork say when he saw identical twins?
They're as alike as toupees in a pod.

Why did the dork go around in the revolving door for three hours?
Because he couldn't remember if he was coming or going.

* * * * * * *

What do you get if you cross a dork with a wristwatch?
A slow clock.

* * * * * * * *

Then there was the dork scientist who thought he'd get rich by inventing an egg with an unbreakable shell.

Why did the dork couple take French lessons?
Because they adopted a French baby and wanted to understand what she said when she began to talk.

* * * * * * * * * * * * * * * * * * *

FOOTBALL COACH: WHY IS IT IMPORTANT NOT TO LOSE YOUR HEAD IN A CLOSE GAME?
DORK PLAYER: BECAUSE THEN I'D HAVE NO PLACE TO PUT MY HELMET.

Mr. Ugly: Doc, every morning when I wake up I look in the mirror and get sick to my stomach. What's wrong with me?
Doctor: I don't know, but your eyesight's perfect.

Mr. Ugly: Doc, did you check out my family tree?
Doctor: Yes. You're the sap.

MR. UGLY: I KNOW I'M NOT HANDSOME. MY PROFILE IS POSTED ON UGLY FACEBOOK.

• •

Mr. Ugly: I know I'm not handsome. A poison control center uses photos of my face to induce vomiting.

• •

Mr. Ugly: I know I'm not handsome. A Halloween mask company wanted to trademark my face.

TRICK OR TREAT!

• • • • • • • • • •

Mr. Ugly: I went to a plastic surgeon. He told me there was no hope for me. I was terminally ugly.

• •

Tino: Dad! Gino called me freaky.
Dad: Gino. Tell your brother you're sorry.
Gino: I'm sorry you're freaky, Tino.

Zack: I went to see the play you wrote and it had a wonderful effect on me.
Mack: Really?
Zack: Yes. It completely cured my insomnia.

• • • • • • • • • • • • • • • • • • • •

WHY DID THE DORK TATTOO WATCHES ON HIS PALMS? BECAUSE HE WANTED TO HAVE FREE TIME ON HIS HANDS.

• • • • • • • • • • • • • • • • • • • •

Why did the dork poultry farmer go broke?
The roosters he bought didn't lay any eggs.

• • • • • • • • • • • • • • • • • • • •

Why did the dork put a hole in her umbrella?
So she could see when it stopped raining.

WHAT DO DORK HELICOPTERS HAVE FOR
PILOTS THAT NO OTHER HELICOPTERS HAVE?
EJECTION SEATS.

How does a dork cheat on an
oral exam?
He sits behind the smartest kid
in class so he can copy.

Why did the five dorks fall off a cliff?
They were playing follow the leader.

What did the dork athlete say when a
pro team offered him a contract for
zero pay?
Triple your offer and you've got a deal.

What game do dorks like to play?
Hide and geek.

What game do baby dorks like
to play?
Geek-a-boo.

WHY DID THE DORK PARK HIS CAR IN FRONT OF THE STOP SIGN?
HE WAS WAITING FOR IT TO CHANGE TO GO.

What did the girls say when she saw a geek at her front door?
Gee, it's dork outside.

How does a dork back up a car?
He looks behind him, puts the car in drive and steps on the gas pedal.

What's the difference between a dork using a handkerchief and a dork using a napkin?
After a dork blows his nose in a handkerchief, it goes back in his pocket. After he blows his nose in a napkin, it goes back on the table.

HOW DID THE DORK HURT HIMSELF
MAKING A BUNGEE JUMP?
HE TIED HIS 200-FOOT ELASTIC CORD
TO A 150-FOOT HIGH BRIDGE.

How did the dork
plan to travel from California
to Hawaii without spending
any money?
He was going to hitchhike all
the way.

How does a dork cook spaghetti?
He throws it on the barbecue.

* *

HOW DOES A DORK MAKE HIS
MARK IN THE WORLD?
HE WRITES GRAFFITI ON A GLOBE.

* *

Why did the dork stay up all night
studying history?
She had an English exam in the
morning.

Do most geeks have blond hair?
No. They have dork hair.

Chester: Have I told you the joke about the deaf man and the dork?
Lester: No. Tell it.
Chester: Huh? What did you say?

How does a dork score in a soccer game?
She picks up the ball and runs over the goal line.

• • • • • • • • • • • • •

What do you get when you clone a dork?
Double dips.

* * * * * * * * * * * * * *

GIRL: WHY DO YOU HAVE BRUISES ON THE SIDES OF YOUR FACE?
DORK: I'VE BEEN TEACHING MYSELF TO PLAY PIANO BY EAR.

When did the dork learn the difference between bowling and soccer?
When he tried to kick a bowling ball.

• • • • • • • • • • • • • • • • • • •

What do you call a dork lizard?
A Geeko.

• • • • • • • • • • • • • • • • • • •

HOW MANY DORKS DOES IT TAKE TO SHOOT A BASKETBALL?
TWO. ONE TO TOSS THE BALL IN THE AIR AND ONE TO FIRE THE SHOTGUN.

• •

How did the dork sink his canoe?
He cut a hole in the bottom so he could watch the fish.

• • • • • • • • • • • • • • • • • • • •

Where does a dork jogger go to run in the Boston Marathon?
New York City.

WHY DID THE DORK SHOWER IN
HIS CLOTHING?
BECAUSE THE TAGS READ "WASH
AND WEAR."

How does a geek soldier check a
field for land mines?
He uses a sledgehammer.

Man: You have your shoes on the wrong feet.
Dork: But these are the only feet I have.

What do you call a geek
on a pier?
The dork of the bay.

How did the dork sink his submarine?
He opened a window to let in some fresh
air while submerged.

WHEN DOES A DORK GO TO BED?
WHEN HE'S NINCOMPOOPED.

Tillie: Why are you standing in front of a mirror with your eyes shut?
Millie: I want to see what I look like when I'm asleep.

Chester: I just bought a suit that came with two pairs of pants, but I don't like it.
Lester: Why not?
Chester: It gets hot wearing two pairs of pants.

WHO IS THE WORLD'S DUMBEST DETECTIVE?

DORK TRACY.

TWO WAY WRIST YO-YO

Tina: You should start saving money now.

Gina: Why?

Tina: It might be worth something someday.

Why did the dork bury pictures of his relatives?
He wanted to grow a family tree.

Why did the dork put a duck under his mattress?
So it could swim in the Spring.

What do geeks wear to see better?
Dork glasses.

Why did the dork put burned bread in the blender?
He wanted to drink a toast.

CHAPTER

8

Stingers

If your I.Q. were ten points higher you'd be a rock.

* * * * * * * * * * * * *

IF HE HAS A CHIP ON HIS SHOULDER, IT'S A SPLINTER FROM THAT BLOCK OF WOOD ABOVE IT.

* * * * * * * * * * * * *

He's so dumb he thinks hotdogs can have puppies.

* * * * * * * * * * * * * * * * *

If ignorance is bliss, he's the world's happiest guy.

* * * * * * * * * * * * * * * * * *

YOUR FEET ARE SO BIG YOU HAVE TO WEAR SUITCASES FOR SHOES.

* * * * * * * * * * * * * *

An intelligent thought doesn't last long in his brain. It can't stand the solitary confinement.

He's so dumb someone told him to call 911 and he started shouting, "9-1-1! 9-1-1!"

****

You're a haunting beauty. You have a face people boo.

****

I HEARD A MEAN WIZARD PUT A SPELL ON YOUR FACE. AND WHAT HE SPELLED IS U.G.L.Y.

****

Hey guess what? I saw clowns at a circus last night and somebody stole your face.

HE NEEDS TO EXERCISE HIS BRAIN MORE. MAYBE THEN HE WOULDN'T BE SUCH A FATHEAD.

It's no wonder you're the teacher's pet. With a face like that you belong on a leash.

You went to beauty school and got expelled.

I heard you had a walk-on part in the *Lord of the Rings* movies. Which Orc were you?

* *

You're so weak you couldn't whip cream.

• •

The last time he went to the zoo, the monkeys threw peanuts at *him*.

WHEN YOU JOINED THE ARMY, THE DRILL SERGEANT YELLED, "ABOUT FACE ... YOURS IS TOO UGLY TO LOOK AT."

Help keep America beautiful. Don't show your face in public.

• •

Aren't you a famous movie actor? Didn't you star in *Toy Story* as Mr. Potato Head?

• •

You're so ugly when someone asks your parents which one of them you resemble, they flip a coin and the loser says "me."

• •

You have a strange growth on your neck. I think it's your head.

• •

You're so ugly, the last mosquito that tried to bite your face died of a heart attack.

YOU'RE SO DUMB THE ONLY TIME YOU HAVE SOMETHING ON YOUR MIND IS WHEN YOU WEAR A HAT.

• •

A movie producer wants to buy the rights to your life story. It's going to make a great horror flick.

• •

His family urged him to pursue a life of crime ... just so he'd wear a mask over his face.

• •

SHE HAD TO STOP TALKING TO HER PLANTS. HER BREATH WAS SO BAD IT MADE THEM WILT.

Your smile reminds me of the Old West ... lots of wide-open spaces.

~~~~~~~~~~~~~~~~~~~~~~~~~~

You're a brave man. It takes a lot of guts to walk around in public with a face like that.

~~~~~~~~~~~~~~~~~~~~~~~~~~

You're so dumb your parents tattooed your name on your arm so you won't forget it.

~~~~~~~~~~~~~~~~~~~~~~~~~~

He's so lazy that waking up in the morning makes him tired.

~~~~~~~~~~~~~~~~~~~~~~~~~~

I MIGHT HAVE A FACE THAT COULD STOP A CLOCK, BUT YOUR FACE GAVE FATHER TIME A HEART ATTACK.

Your eyes remind me of two cool pools of water ... dirty dishwater.

Did you come by your looks naturally or did a doctor prescribe ugly pills for you as a child?

YOU'RE THE ONLY PERSON I KNOW WHO CAN MAKE FUNNY FACES WITHOUT EVEN TRYING.

You're so ugly that if they made your life story into a movie, it would be a horror flick.

NOW SHOWING

THE HORROR!

Every time I look at your face I get the feeling you're about to say trick or treat.

With a face like yours, you should be thankful mirrors don't come with an automatic laugh track.

If ugliness were a crime, your face would be a felony.

Is that your head or did someone find a way to grow hair on a meatball?

HIS B.O. IS SO BAD THE TEACHER GAVE HIM AN AUTOMATIC A IN CLASS PARTICIPATION SO WOULDN'T HAVE TO RAISE HIS HAND.

You don't need a gun to go hunting. You just walk through the woods and your face scares wild animals to death.

They looked up his family tree and discovered he's nothing but dead wood.

YOUR MOM IS AN AWFUL COOK. SHE'S THE ONLY PERSON I KNOW WHO CAN BURN ICE CREAM.

He's so unpopular. Yesterday at breakfast his talking cereal called him a name.

Talk about ugly. I've seen better heads on pimples.

What's the name of the perfume you're wearing, ode de skunk?

You're really dumb. The last time you had a brainstorm it was nothing but a drizzle.

****

I DREAMED ABOUT YOU LAST NIGHT. MY MOTHER WARNED ME IF I ATE A SNACK BEFORE BEDTIME I'D HAVE NIGHTMARES.

****

I've seen nicer hairstyles on old mops.

****

Your I.Q. is so low you misspelled I.Q.

****

BIG FOOT JUST CALLED FOR YOU. HE WANTS HIS FEET BACK.

Oh, you're a bad dude all right. Bad Breath. Bad Odor. And bad looking.

• •

I'd try to read your mind if the print wasn't so tiny.

• •

We'd like a breath of fresh air, so please hold yours.

• •

What are you doing here? Was there a jailbreak at the zoo?

• •

DOES YOUR MOTHER KNOW YOU'RE OUT HERE WITHOUT YOUR LEASH?

Help beautify America! Don't show your face in public.

The American Medical Association should give you a yearly bonus. Your face makes people sick.

HE HAS A LOT OF BLIND DATES. THE ONLY GIRLS WHO WILL GO OUT WITH HIM ARE ONE WHO CAN'T SEE HIS FACE.

▲▲▲▲▲▲▲▲▲▲▲▲▲▲▲▲▲▲▲▲▲▲▲▲▲▲▲▲▲▲

When you took your Army I.Q. test, you qualified for training in the K-9 Corps.

▼▼▼▼▼▼▼▼▼▼▼▼▼▼▼▼▼▼▼▼▼▼▼▼▼▼▼▼▼▼

Your face is as pretty as a flower ... a cauliflower.

Did I hear you singing or was someone torturing a cat?

I heard you had to go in for a checkup. What did the vet have to say?

Your life has been a real trip, and it looks like you fell on your face.

▼▼▼▼▼▼▼▼▼▼▼▼▼▼▼▼

IS THAT YOUR HEAD OR DID SOMEONE FIND A WAY TO GROW HAIR ON A WATERMELON?

▲▲▲▲▲▲▲▲▲▲▲▲▲▲▲▲

Your brother is so dumb that he saw the word "race" on his job application and ran out of the room.

▼▼▼▼▼▼▼▼▼▼▼▼▼▼▼▼

Your grandparents are so old they studied ancient history when it was called current events.

WHERE DO YOU DIG UP YOUR DATES?
A CEMETERY?

Is that your nose or are you eating a banana?

If I were married to your aunt, I'd be a monkey's uncle.

You've always been ugly. When you were born the doctor slapped your parents.

You're so old you knew the Garden of Eden when it was a seed farm.

Guys like you don't grow on trees. They swing from them.

YOU SHOULD VISIT THE ZOO MORE OFTEN. I'M SURE YOUR RELATIVES WOULD BE GLAD TO SEE YOU.

Everyone thought you were a marvel of science until they discovered you were a boy instead of a talking chimp.

CHAPTER **9**

Funny Things

What did the
clock shout on
its birthday?
It's party time!

****

What did the tired rubber band say to the sofa?
I think I'll stretch out on you.

****

What did the wristwatch say to
the lost travel clock?
How did you wind up here?

****

WHAT DO YOU GET IF YOU CROSS
ROCKS AND CLOCKS?
HARD TIMES.

What do you get if you cross a car
tire and a poker player?
A wheeler dealer.

What do you call a wager between ABC and XYZ?
An alpha-bet.

• •

WHY IS A PIANO AN EXPERT ON LOCKS?
BECAUSE IT HAS LOTS OF KEYS.

• •

What do you get when you cross super glue with a novel?
A book you can't put down.

• •

How do you make a V-6 car go faster?
Give it a V-8.

• •

What did one doorknob say to the other?
Wait for your turn.

• •

What gets wetter the more it dries?
A towel.

What did the cup say to the sad coffee maker?
Perk up.

· ·

WHAT DID THE ANGRY PAINTBRUSH SAY TO THE FLOOR?
ONE MORE WISE REMARK AND I'LL SHELLAC YOU.

· · · · · · · · · · · · ·

What do you get when a dollar bill loses its temper?
Mad money.

· ·

Why did the clock go jogging?
He was running late that day.

What do you get if you cross a car and a garden?
A Ford plant.

WHAT DID ONE COMPACT SAY TO THE OTHER?
YOU ALWAYS MAKE UP STORIES.

* * * * * * * * * * * * * * *

What did the doctor say to the sick pot of glue?
Stick out your tongue.

WHAT DO YOU GET IF YOU CROSS A FAST CAR AND A CAMERA?
A ZOOM-ZOOM LENS.

Why did the oil well make a mess?
It was crude oil.

* *

What did the driller say to the oil well?
Come on. Spill your guts.

WHAT DID THE PENCIL SAY TO THE PAPER?
I DOT MY I'S ON YOU.

* * * * * * * * * * * * * * * * * *

Dolly: How much does this bottle
of glue cost?
Molly: Check the sticker price.

How do you keep a bus from going
down the bathtub drain?
Put in a bus stopper.

How
can you
change a
flat tire
with a
deck of
cards?
Take out
the jack.

* * * * * * * * * * * * * * * * * *

What did one lipstick say to the other?
Let's kiss and make up.

What happened to the nervous crepe paper?
It became unraveled.

What happened when
the glue went to the fruit stand?
It got stuck with a lemon.

WHAT DO YOU CALL A PIANO WHOSE
CHILDREN HAVE CHILDREN?
A GRAND PIANO.

* *

What do you get if you cross
fifty-two cards and a stool?
A deck chair.

• •

Dan: That cruise ship must love
the coastline.
Van: What makes you say that?
Dan: It's hugging the shore.

* *

WHAT DID THE ENVELOPE SAY TO THE PEN?
WERE YOU ADDRESSING ME?

What did the
tennis racket
ask the
tennis ball?
Do you mind if
I court you?

****

What has a hundred legs but can't walk?
Fifty pairs of pants.

****

What kind of dolls sing in harmony?
A Barbie shop quartet.

****

Why was the tornado so proud?
It set a whirl record.

Why did the newspaper have a
mild heart attack?
It had poor circulation.

MRS. JONES: WHAT DO YOU THINK OF PAPER PLATES?

MRS. SMITH: THEY'RE TEARABLE.

• • • • • • • • • • • • • • • • • • • •

SIGN ON A DEAD BATTERY-
Free, no charge.

• • • • • • • • • • • • • • • • • • • •

What kind of hat has lots of fingerprints on it?

A felt hat.

• • • • • • • • • • • • • •

WHERE DOES A PIECE OF SOD SIT? IN A LAWN CHAIR.

• • • • • • • • • • • • • • • • • • •

What do you call an intelligent crevice? A wisecrack.

What happens when a shy rock grows up?
It becomes boulder.

Knock! Knock!
Who's there?
Esteem.
Esteem who?
Esteem locomotive goes
choo, choo!

Why was the little milk container so bad?
His parents spoiled him.

Why was Mrs. Plate so upset?
She came from a dishfunctional
family.

BOY: WHAT DOES YOUR WATCH SAY?
GIRL: TICK TOCK! TICK TOCK!

Gina: **Why are Mr. and Mrs. Three so happy?**
Nina: **They're going to have a little one.**

John: **This is my cheesy watch.**
Lon: **Why do you call it that?**
John: **Because it's Swiss.**

MRS. PASTE: DID YOU MAKE A GLUE YEAR'S RESOLUTION?
MR. PASTE: YES, BUT I DON'T THINK I'LL STICK TO IT.

What did the trunk say to the broken suitcase?
You need to get a grip on yourself.

When does a wallet get a wedgie?
When money is tight.

What's the best way to mail a bird's egg?
Use nest day delivery.

WHAT DO YOU CALL A TINY CELL PHONE?
A MICRO PHONE.

Why didn't Mr. Zombie's car start?
It had a dead battery.

Why didn't the
wristwatch
make the
track team?
It ran
too slow.

CAN'T KEEP UP WITH THE OLD MAN, EH?

**What did the
jack say to
the flat tire?
Can I give you a lift?**

WHAT HAPPENED TO THE SNOW
TIRES THE YETI PUT ON HIS CAR?
THEY MELTED.

What kinds of clocks make great wide receivers?
Ones that have good hands.

* *

What do all golf carts have?
Fore-wheel drive.

* *

What did one cowboy pea say to the other?
Howdy Podner.

What do you get if you cross morning mist with a pastry chef?
Dewnuts.

When do two soda cans get engaged? After one pops the question.

What do vegetables yell when the farmer wants to play a game?
Pick me! Pick me!

WHAT DO YOU TRY TO KEEP AFTER GIVING IT TO SOMEONE ELSE?
A PROMISE.

What kind of car does a rich golfer drive?
A Caddylac.

* *

What did the police shade say to the drapes?
Watch out for the curtains, they're carrying a rod.

WHAT KIND OF SHOE TALKS TOO MUCH?
ONE THAT HAS A TONGUE THAT WAGS.

● ●

What did the teen calendar
ask her parents?
Am I old enough to go out on
dates alone?

● ●

Where does a broom scout nap on a campout?
In a sweeping bag.

● ●

CHAPTER
10
Silly Sentences

Drink this medicine encase you feel sick.

AFTER THE PARTY OUR HOUSE WAS AMASS.

That low price is asbestos I can do.

Adjust don't care what you do.

This is the warship I ever sailed on.

OPEN FIRE SOLDIERS. IT'S USHER THEM!

If you drink a glass of warm milk, you will go to sleep the miniature in bed.

My jeans have ripped knees, but no tears on deceit.

If a boy comes over to your house, you'd better vitamin or he'll go home mad.

Teenagers should show proper respect folder people.

The reason I came on *Wheel of Fortune* is because I want to window.

YOUR PRIZE!

WIN!

AFTER YOU HIT A BASEBALL YOU HAVE TORONTO FIRST BASE.

Guess what? I avenue baby brother.

Mount Everest is so high you have to be a little crazy to climate.

THE PRESIDENT DECIDED TO COMMUTER SENTENCE.

* *

WHEN A CAT IS VERY THIRSTY ELAPSE UP ALL OF HIS MILK.

You can go to college, but festival you have to graduate from high school.

• •

Those shoes are nice, but have you tried ammonia to see if they fit right?

The marshal got in a shootout with some outlaws and now he has a bulletin his arm.

The patient is doing well thanks to the curious taking now.

Why did you get insulate last night?

THE FODDER YOU JOG THE MORE
TIRED YOU GET.

• •

You supply the frankfurters
and I'll bring a Canada best
sauerkraut money can buy.

**Take this Madison and you'll feel
better soon.**

* *

I'M HUNGRY.
LET'S GOPHER
A PIZZA.

PIZZA

• • • • • • • • • • • • • • • • • • •

The way to win a prize at a game
of chance is to piccolo number.

I stay home because symptoms I don't feel like going out.

I felt terrific yesterday, but today adjust don't feel so hot.

• •

The lady's pet chimp grabbed her hand embitter on the finger.

THE TREE IN MY BACKYARD IS SO TALL I CAN'T CLIMATE.

• •

My father likes to relax in front of his TV on the daisies off from work.

I AVENUE JOB AS AN ENGLISH TEACHER.

Rebus hurry or we'll miss the train.

● ● ● ● ● ● ● ● ● ● ● ● ● ● ● ● ● ● ● ●

**Going on carnival
rides symptoms makes
me dizzy.**

YOUR KITCHEN FLOURISH KIND OF DIRTY.

● ● ● ● ● ● ● ● ● ● ● ● ● ● ● ● ● ● ● ●

I Santa letter home to your parents.

When you bet cash on a horserace,
sometimes you window.

● ● ● ● ● ● ● ● ● ● ● ● ● ● ● ● ● ● ● ●

**The bull wouldn't go in the barn,
but the coward.**

● ● ● ● ● ● ● ● ● ● ● ● ● ● ● ● ● ●

The surfer who wiped out yelled, "Alp! Alp!
I'm drowning!"

This old tugboat is the worship I've ever been on.

THE FOREMAN TOLD US TO LOATHSOME CRATES ON THE TRUCK.

My lazy teenage son satyr all day playing video games.

Pick that paper off the floor and commonplace it in the trashcan.

IF YOU PLANT BULBS IN SEPTEMBER IN JUNIOR FLOWERS WILL GROW.

My brother didn't want the last pancake so I edit.

London an airplane takes a lot of practice.

Your ankle looks fine, but does journey hurt?

I've been garden the prisoner all night, Marshal.

The teacher told me to open my ears and to clothes my mouth.

SWIMMING FIVE LAPS IN THE POOL IS ASBESTOS I CAN DO.

Jack and Jill were cistern brother.

If your blankets are too short, your fiddlestick out.

* * * * * * * * * * * * * * * * * *

Yes, we do currently have a room toilet.

FOR RENT

* *

Here, drink this encase you feel seasick.

THE ARMY DOCTOR SAID, "SEND IN TUMOR MEN."

Mr. Jones walks around with a stiff neck because he's afraid his wiggle fall off.

Joe got caught on barbed wire and tourist pants.

When you change Judy's diaper sprinkler with baby powder.

The gym teacher said Billy and I make quite a pear.

* * * * * * * * * * * * * * * * * *

Absent a letter to my Aunt June.

CHAPTER
11
Last Laughs

What has big antlers and lives in Disney World?
Mickey Moose.

• • • • • • • • • • • •

Benny: Do you know how the ten-cent fairy tale begins?

Jenny: No.

Benny: Once upon a dime ...

• • • • • • • • • • • • • • • • • • • •

KEN: I ONCE SANG THE STAR SPANGLED BANNER FOR TWO HOURS.

LEN: BIG DEAL. I CAN SING STARS AND STRIPES FOREVER.

• • • • • • • • • • • • • • • • • • • •

What do you get if you cross the Loch Ness Monster with a great white shark?
Loch Jaw.

THE DAFFY DIFFERENCE BETWEEN YOUNG & OLD:

... When you're young, you love birthdays. They don't come soon enough. When you're old, you hate birthdays and wish they'd never arrive.

• •

... When you're young, you're positive old people don't know what they're talking about. When you're old, you're positive young people don't know what they're talking about.

• •

... When you're young, getting up early is a drag. When you're old, you drag yourself upstairs to go to bed early.

• •

... When you're young, you wish Christmas came more than once a year. When you're old, you're glad Christmas only comes once a year because you can't afford it.

Pilot: I'm not sure I can fly a plane as well as I used to.
Navigator: Try taking off a few days.

Investor: I don't mind that my money doesn't go far today. What troubles me is that it doesn't stay put.

What do you say to
a baby wearing
designer jeans?
Gucci, Gucci, Gucci!

Show me a developer who makes all of his deals on the side of a hill ... and I'll show you a real estate agent who is not on the level.

How can you find out how long a printing press is?
Use a type measurer.

WHAT IS LASSIE'S FAVORITE STATE?
COLLIERADO.

****

What is Lassie's second most favorite state.

Colliefornia.

****

FARMER #1: I WAS EXPECTING TEN YOUNG CHICKENS AND MY HENS HATCHED OUT ELEVEN.

FARMER #2: CONGRATULATIONS! YOU GOT A BONUS CHICK!

****

What famous love story did Santa Claus write?

Romeo Ho Ho and Juliet.

Farmer: I'd like to buy a rooster and two hens and charge it.
Clerk: Yes, sir. Do you have a chicken account with us?

Sally: Why won't you date Mr. Magnet?

Kelly: His looks repel me.

• •

SIGN ON A BLANKET FACTORY: Come in and look around. There's no cover charge.

* *

ATTENTION:

Ms. Perfume Bottle has no scents.
Mr. Scissors can't cut it any longer.
Mr. Knife is a sharp dresser.
Mr. Paste sticks to his story.

Ms. Plate is a hot dish.
Mr. Straw knows how to suck it up.

• •

BORK: I WON THE INTERNATIONAL BURPING
CONTEST AGAIN THIS YEAR.
DORK: I GUESS THAT MAKES YOU A REPEAT
CHAMPION.

● ●

Cabin Boy: Why is that pirate
guarding the treasure?
Captain: He's our chest protector.

● ●

**Girl: Mom. Johnny has a filthy
mouth.
Mother: What do you mean? What
did your little brother say?
Girl: Nothing. He's been eating
mud pies.**

● ●

WHAT DO YOU CALL A FARMER
WHO RAISES SHEEP?
A SHEAR CROPPER.

● ●

Show me a dork who swallows dynamite
... and I'll show you a guy who's going to
get a bang out of life.

What is the favorite music of Irish teenagers?
Shamrock.

• •

What does a dogcatcher play golf with?
Kennel clubs.

• •

Judge: Do not tell any jokes in my courtroom, counselor.
Attorney: Is that a gag order, your honor?

• •

What's green, yodels and has holes?
Irish Swiss Cheese.

• •

ATHLETE: I'D LIKE TO INSURE MY TENNIS SERVE.
AGENT: ALL WE OFFER IS NO FAULT INSURANCE.

Sharon: I got a new puppy for my boyfriend.
Karen: That sounds like a good trade to me.

Knock! Knock!
Who's there?
Scold.
Scold who?
Scold outside so dress warm.

VAGRANT: IF I KNEW HOW TO MAKE MONEY I WOULDN'T BE IN JAIL.
COUNTERFEITER: I KNEW HOW TO MAKE MONEY AND THAT'S WHY I'M IN HERE.

****
What do you get if you cross an untidy hobo with a millionaire? A guy who is filthy rich.

Jed: I keep my retirement money hidden in an old pot.
Fred: I have a pension pan.

- -

Boss: Did you men build that rickety staircase?
Carpenter: Yes, sir, but it won't happen again.
Boss: Okay. But from now on watch your steps.

- -

What did the mosquitoes say after they flew off of Robinson Crusoe?
Let's get together again on Friday.

- - - - - - - - - - - - - - - -

OLD KING COLE WAS A MERRY OLD SOLE UNTIL HE WAS HOOKED BY A FISHERMAN.

* * * * * * * * * * * * * * * *

What fish lives in Washington, DC?
The Senate Herring.

I YIELD THE FLOOR TO THE GENTLEMAN FROM LAKE MICHIGAN!

"I've got to find a way to blow off some steam," Robert Fulton.

• •

"Oh go fly a kite!" Mr. Franklin to his son Ben.

• •

"Writing this poem is making me a raven maniac!" Edgar Allen Poe.

• •

"I've got a code in my head," Samuel Morse.

• •

"Some girls lose their heads over me," King Henry the Eighth.

"You boys are both airheads," **Mrs. Wright to her sons Orville and Wilber.**

• •

"What a revolting development this is," King George of England in 1776."

• •

"There's a hot time in the old town tonight," Nero.

THE WINDY PAPER LAW · If the wind blows papers off your desk and out the window, important papers will be lost forever and useless junk will land near the desk.

THE PIZZA LAW – The place that makes the best pizza is located the farthest from your house and does not deliver.

THE RAINCOAT LAW · Your raincoat can only be found on sunny days.

• •

THE DOG LAW – Your pet dog never has to go out at night until you're ready to go to bed.

• • • • • • • • • • • • • •

THE ICE CREAM LAW·
Your sister's ice cream cone always lasts longer than the one you're eating.

• •

THE PRODUCT LAW–
Easy-to-assemble products come with tons of instructions. Hard-to-assemble items come with no instructions.

• •

THE TV LAW · The cable always goes out just before the big game or your favorite program starts.

THE SHOE LAW- The best looking shoes in the store don't come in your size.

● ● ● ● ● ● ● ● ● ● ● ● ● ●

THE SCHOOL PARENTS LAW · Back to School Night is always held on the evening of a sporting event you're dying to watch.

● ● ● ● ● ● ● ● ● ● ● ● ● ● ● ● ● ● ● ●

THE BUS LAW – School buses only break down on the way home from school.

● ● ● ● ● ● ● ● ● ● ● ● ● ● ● ● ● ● ● ●

THE LIGHT LAW · Your flashlight always works fine until there's a blackout or a power failure.

THE TOY LAW – The most expensive toys break easily. The cheap toys last forever.

* * * * * * * * * * * * * * *

SNOW LAW · You wake up and rejoice because a blizzard has dumped ten feet of snow on the ground and school is sure to be cancelled. Then you realize winter break started.

* * * * * * * * * * * * * * *

SCHOOL LAW #1 – On the exam the teacher always asks the one question you didn't study because you figured she'd never ask it.

* * * * * * * * * * * * * * * * * *

SCHOOL LAW #2 · The principal always sees the kid who hits second and not the kid who hits first.

* * * * * * * * * * * * * * *

DOGGIE DIRT LAW – your pet will always roll in the dirt just minutes after you give it a bath.

DATING LAW– Pretty girls always have strict fathers and big, tough brothers.

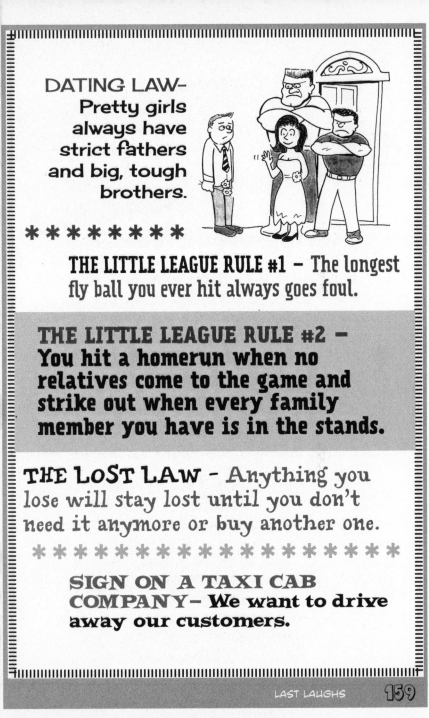

* * * * * * * *

THE LITTLE LEAGUE RULE #1 – The longest fly ball you ever hit always goes foul.

THE LITTLE LEAGUE RULE #2 – You hit a homerun when no relatives come to the game and strike out when every family member you have is in the stands.

THE LOST LAW - Anything you lose will stay lost until you don't need it anymore or buy another one.

* * * * * * * * * * * * * * * * * *

SIGN ON A TAXI CAB COMPANY– We want to drive away our customers.